God's *Gift for* Mothers

Published by
THOMAS NELSON™
Since 1798

www.thomasnelson.com

Nashville Dallas Mexico City Rio De Janeiro Beijing

Published in Nashville, TN, by Thomas Nelson.
Thomas Nelson is a trademark of Thomas Nelson, Inc.

Thomas Nelson, Inc., titles may be purchased in bulk for educational,
business, fundraising, or sales promotional use. For information,
please email SpecialMarkets@ThomasNelson.com.

All scripture references are from the *New King James Version of the Bible* (NKJV) ©1979,
1980, 1982, 1992, Thomas Nelson, Inc., Publisher. All rights reserved.

Designed by Blackbird Creative

ISBN: 978–14041–8668–9

Printed in the United States of America

Contents

Preface

A mother is a precious gift to her family. She's a nurturer, a teacher, a ringleader, a friend. She's the one who makes a house a home.

Mothers fill their days with caring for their families in every way. They taxi the kids, wipe little noses, keep the madhouse running smoothly (or at least running), and make sure everyone is fed and clothed and educated and loved. They often work outside the home or volunteer with schools or churches or other organizations. They make time for their husbands and sometimes even for themselves.

Mothers are, indeed, remarkable women. They're priceless gifts from God.

Mothers must lovingly give so much to their families, so our wise heavenly Father has bestowed some of His best gifts on them. He's promised mothers His presence and His provision. He's offered His wisdom for every circumstance and emotion of life.

Dear mother, this little book is for you. It's filled with refreshment from the Word of God as well as insights to encourage your heart and uplift your spirit.

You are a gift to your family. Let these words be a gift of encouragement to you.

Abide

I am the vine, you are the branches.
He who abides in Me, and I in him, bears much fruit;
for without Me you can do nothing.
<small>JOHN 15:5</small>

When a mother chooses to abide in the Lord, she will infect her entire family with His love and create a bond that will enrich her life and bless her marriage.

Ability

*If anyone speaks, let him speak as the oracles
of God. If anyone ministers, let him do it
as with the ability which God supplies, that in
all things God may be glorified through
Jesus Christ, to whom belong the glory and
the dominion forever and ever.*

1 PETER 4:11

*G*od places within the heart of each mother the ability to nurture others. He does not give your specific intuition and instincts to anyone else. Pray for God's guidance that you may fulfill the calling He has given you to the best of your abilities.

Abound

And God is able to make all grace abound
toward you, that you, always having
all sufficiency in all things, may have an
abundance for every good work.
2 CORINTHIANS 9:8

The word *abound* is such a strong
expression of action that if you, as a
mother, abound in your love for your
family, there will be a reflection of love
that will be contagious for everyone to see.

Above

Every good gift and every perfect gift is from above,
and comes down from the Father of lights, with whom
there is no variation or shadow of turning.
JAMES 1:17

A mother's journey will present many different situations that you must learn to accept and deal with. Just remember that God uses all of these situations to create opportunities for you to grow and be more complete for His glory.

Abstain

*Beloved, I beg you as sojourners
and pilgrims, abstain from fleshly lusts
which war against the soul.*
1 PETER 2:11

How you live as a mother is so important to those you love and care for the most. Abstain from anything that would destroy your marriage and bring dishonor to your family. God has given you a precious gift. Cherish what He has given you without reservation.

Abundance

The very core of being a mother is found in the heart of God. If your desire to be a mother has grown stale, ask God to give you an abundance of the love He so generously gives to those who ask Him. It's still true: ask and you shall receive. Accept His generous offer of love today for you and your family.

Acceptable to God

Walk as children of light . . .
finding out what is acceptable to the Lord.
And have no fellowship with the unfruitful works
of darkness, but rather expose them.
EPHESIANS 5:8, 10–11

The way we live in the eyes of God will also be what our children see. Learn to be a great role model that leaves no doubt in your children's minds how they should conduct themselves in all circumstances.

Acceptable to Family

*(For the fruit of the Spirit is in all goodness,
righteousness, and truth), finding out
what is acceptable to the Lord. And have
no fellowship with the unfruitful works
of darkness, but rather expose them.*
EPHESIANS 5:9–11

$\mathcal{L}$earning what is acceptable to your mate
and teaching those principles to your children
is one of the great responsibilities of
motherhood. Let God, through His Spirit,
guide you to become everything He wishes
for you as a mother.

Accord

Again I say to you that if two of you
agree on earth concerning anything that
they ask, it will be done for them
by My Father in heaven.

MATTHEW 18:19

Two hearts don't always beat as one.
However, in important matters of your life
together, seek harmony with everyone in
your family. You will then be able to
experience the joy of life with agreement and
a deep sense of meaning and purpose.

Acknowledge

Trust in the LORD with all your heart,
And lean not on your own understanding;
In all your ways acknowledge Him,
And He shall direct your paths.
PROVERBS 3:5–6

As God directs us to trust and acknowledge Him in all our ways, it is important that we do the same with each member of the family. When every member of a family is trusting in the Lord, they experience a bond that cannot be broken.

Adoption

*For you did not receive the spirit of bondage
again to fear, but you received the Spirit of adoption by
whom we cry out, "Abba, Father."*
ROMANS 8:15

*A*ll children are heaven sent from God. When you as a
mother receive a child through adoption, it is a unique
and special gift. Praise God for His generosity and love
your children as God so generously loves you.

Affection

For if you love those who love you,
what reward have you? Do not even the tax collectors
do the same?... Therefore you shall be perfect,
just as your Father in heaven is perfect.
MATTHEW 5:46, 48

Be patient in your love. Don't insist on returning a harsh word that has been spoken. Don't always try to make the last parting shot in an argument. Love those in your family even when they are not acting in love.

Afraid

Behold, God is my salvation.
I will trust and not be afraid;
"For YAH, the LORD, is my strength and song;
He also has become my salvation."
ISAIAH 12:2

*F*ear is a killer for any marriage. Do not let that evil viper enter your household. God has promised He will never leave you or forsake you. Claim that promise today.

Almighty

The Spirit of God has made me,
And the breath of the Almighty gives me life.
JOB 33:4

When a mother learns to recognize that God Almighty is the answer to peace and contentment within her own life, the responsibility of being a wife and mother will be as clear as crystal because the Almighty wishes to bless you in every way.

Alone

Then they cried out to the LORD
in their trouble,
And He delivered them out of their distresses.
And He led them forth by the right way.
PSALM 107:6–7

If you have problems, don't wait to take them to God. You cannot face your hard times alone. Ask God to intervene and give you wisdom. He will stand with you in each situation. Take all your problems and concerns to the Lord in earnest prayer.

Always

Rejoice in the Lord always.
Again I will say, rejoice!
Let your gentleness be known to all men.
The Lord is at hand.
Philippians 4:4–5

Always is such an all-encompassing word. When a mother is steadfast with those she holds most dear to her heart, it creates a bond that cannot be easily broken. Let your family know you will always be there for them in all circumstances.

Answer

Call to Me, and I will answer you,
and show you great and mighty things,
which you do not know.
JEREMIAH 33:3

As a mother, you will never have all the answers for your children or your husband. But thank God who invites you to call upon Him for guidance and direction in your life.

Appearance

Do not judge according to appearance,
but judge with righteous judgment.
JOHN 7:24

As the queen of her household, a mother's appearance is very important to those she loves. But the appearance of her heart, more than her physical appearance, will speak volumes as her family grows together.

Approval

Love suffers long and is kind; love . . .
does not rejoice in inequity,
but rejoices in the truth.
1 CORINTHIANS 13:4, 6

Truth is a precious gift freely given to you and your family. It is simply yours for the taking. Telling the truth is the key to being known by each other and feeling the wondrous release of being wholly approved of by your loved ones. With true approval lies great peace.

Assurance

Let us draw near with a true heart
in full assurance of faith, having our hearts
sprinkled from an evil conscience
and our bodies washed with pure water.
HEBREWS 10:22

*A*s you celebrate the gift of motherhood, you can have the full assurance that God is truly for you and not against you. He desires that your life be fruitful and full of joy. May you be blessed among all women.

Beauty

My beloved spoke, and said to me:
"Rise up my love, my fair one,
And come away.
For lo, the winter is past,
The rain is over and gone."
SONG OF SOLOMON 2:10–11

*C*ompliments are like a welcome summer
breeze after the gales of winter. Tell your
beloved of the beauty your eyes see. Speak
often of your deep, deep love, and your
relationship will blossom. It's still true you will
reap what you sow. Speak love and you harvest
love. Let your marriage be a trophy of loving.

Beginnings

The angel of the LORD encamps all
around those who fear Him,
And delivers them.
Oh, taste and see that the LORD is good.
PSALM 34:7–8

The beginnings of family life are like a vapor. There may be times when it will seem easier just to let it blow away. But God puts His angels before you and desires to stop the vapor from disappearing. Ask Him to keep your love alive. He wants the best for you and your family as you continue to share your life, living and loving together.

Blessings

"And all nations will call you blessed,
For you will be a delightful land,"
Says the LORD of Hosts.
Malachi 3:12

*W*hen people receive a gift, they usually cannot wait
to tell everyone they know about it. Your children are one
of God's greatest blessings to you. Make sure other people
know of your regard for them. Don't keep their good
qualities a secret. Speak of your blessings to others.

Blossom

So Boaz took Ruth and she became his wife;
and when he went in to her,
the LORD gave her conception, and she bore a son.

RUTH 4:13

As you grow as a mother, ask God to make your love blossom into a tree that shades your life with goodness and contentment. Do not count the cost of love. Look only to its end result.

Center

Delight yourself also in the LORD,
And He shall give you the desires of your heart.
PSALM 37:4

*C*enter your heart around God, and He will give you the desires of your heart. Come to God and dedicate your love to Him. Thank Him for giving you your children and your husband.

Children

Like arrows in the hand of a warrior,
So are the children of one's youth.
PSALM 127:4

*G*od has given you a gift. Your precious
children are created in His image. God
delights in giving you good things. Praise
Him every day for the blessings He has so
generously given you.

Closer

If I take the wings of the morning,
And dwell in the uttermost parts of the sea,
Even there Your hand shall lead me,
And Your right hand shall hold me.
PSALM 139:9–10

$\mathcal{S}$ometimes it may feel like God is painfully far away from you and the ones you hold dear. But in reality, God is near at hand no matter where you are—from the top of the highest mountain to the bottom of the deepest ocean. Remember His promise: "I will never leave you nor forsake you" (Hebrews 13:5). Live in that awareness of His closeness to you.

Comfort

"For the LORD has called you
Like a woman forsaken and grieved in spirit,
Like a youthful wife when you were refused,"
Says your God.
ISAIAH 54:6

*G*od binds up the rejected. If your husband turns from you, know that you will be comforted in the arms of our heavenly Father. He grieves with those who grieve and He comforts all who turn to Him. Rejection is painful, but whatever you endure makes you stronger.

Contagious

Beloved, if God so loved us,
we also ought to love one another.
1 John 4:11

A mother's love is wonderfully contagious. God's loving kindness to you can prompt you to acts of kindness toward your family. Let your whole household be infected with the joy of loving. Spread that joy today—wherever you are and in whatever you do.

Courage

Moreover if your brother sins against you,
go and tell him his fault
between you and him alone.
MATTHEW 18:15

Courage is the tool that sculpts and refines a loving marriage. It takes courage to tell your beloved that you have been hurt by words or deeds. But do not neglect the cleansing of your hurt feelings. If you do, you will fester and injure your love. Have the courage to speak of your feelings—and do it with love in your heart.

Covenant

He remembers His covenant forever,
The word which He commanded,
for a thousand generations.
PSALM 105:8

God has made a commitment to you, your spouse, and your children. If you follow Him, He will remember you and redeem you. Be a gentle guide to your whole family as you yourself follow His counsel today.

Delight

He also brought me out into a broad place;
He delivered me
because He delighted in me.
2 SAMUEL 22:20

$\mathcal{A}$s a mother, pour warm laughter over
your life with your family. Ask the Father
who delights in each of us to teach you to
delight in the ways of each other as children
delight in each new day's discoveries.

Devotion of Praise

LORD, you have been our
dwelling place in all generations.
Before the mountains were brought forth,
Or ever You had formed the earth and the world,
Even from everlasting to everlasting,
You are God.
PSALM 90:1–2

*G*od's hand is the one that fashioned you
and your family—your personalities, your
intelligence, your deepest desires. Rejoice in
His presence in your life together and give
Him your devotion.

Devotion of Study

Blessed are You, O LORD!
Teach me your statutes....
I will meditate on Your precepts,
And contemplate Your ways.
I will delight myself in Your statutes;
I will not forget Your word.

PSALM 119:12, 15–16

$\mathscr{S}$et aside a regular time for you, as a mother, to read God's Word. As your soul grows closer to the soul of God, you will find yourself growing closer to each one in your family. Make shared devotions once a day a vital part of your family relationship and your spiritual growth together.

Discernment

*The secret of the LORD is with those who fear Him,
And He will show them His covenant.*

PSALM 25:14

$\mathcal{N}$ot all ways of the Lord are plain to our earthly eyes. Sometimes the workings of the Father are subtle and can only be observed by the most discerning mind. Seek to know how God is working in your life as a mother.

Dreams

Then God said to Abraham, "As for Sarai your wife,
you shall not call her name Sarai, but Sarah shall
be her name. And I will bless her and also give you a son by
her; then I will bless her and she shall be a
mother of nations; kings of peoples shall be from her."
Genesis 17:15–16

*G*od specializes in new beginnings. In the historic past as much as in the present, God has given new dreams to those who are faithful and has stood with them as their most cherished dreams come true. Don't be afraid to ask God for a new plan for your future.

Emotions

From the end of the earth I will cry to You,
When my heart is overwhelmed;
Lead me to the rock that is higher than I.
For You have been a shelter for me,
A strong tower from the enemy.
PSALM 61:2–3

*A*s a mother, your love relationship is a place for you to know your emotions. Your fears, joys, concerns, hurts, and moments of ecstasy are all a part of the person God made you to be. Celebrate them with all your might.

Encouragement

Therefore comfort each other
and edify one another,
just as you also are doing.
1 THESSALONIANS 5:11

*D*on't comfort your family from a
standpoint of weakness. Be strong. Have
courage. Speak the truth in love. Comfort
them in a way that brings encouragement.
Help build on strengths that already exist.
Remember life has many seasons and troubles
come and go. You always have reasons to hope.

Enthusiasm

*But Jesus said, "Let the little children
come to Me, and do not forbid them; for of
such is the kingdom of heaven."*
MATTHEW 19:14

Don't underestimate your children. The
natural dependency and openness of a child
is so precious that Jesus said it was childlike
people who made up His kingdom.
Encourage your children to keep the
enthusiasm of their early days—so that it
may serve them well as they grow into adults.

Esteem

Let nothing be done through selfish ambition
or conceit, but in lowliness of mind
let each esteem others better than himself.
PHILIPPIANS 2:3

*L*ove is a dance of poetry. The self-esteem that you breathe into your children and spouse will come back to you many times over. When each person is showing love for others, it will sweeten your family's love and make it stronger.

Evening

I call to remembrance my song in the night;
I meditate within my heart,
And my spirit makes diligent search.
PSALM 77:6

After the sun has set and darkness covers your face, seek the sweet communion of time spent with your family at the merciful throne of your Father. He will give you comfort in times of trial and sustenance when the challenges seem too great. Believe in His great mercy today.

Example

Blessed is the man
Who walks not in the counsel of the ungodly,
Nor stands in the path of sinners,
Nor sits in the seat of the scornful;
But his delight is in the law of the LORD,
And in His law he meditates day and night.

PSALM 1:1–2

If you want your children to grow up to be God-fearing men or women, then you and your mate need to show them what God-fearing people live like. There is no substitute for a loving example. Be that example of God's love today.

Focus

O God, my heart is steadfast;
I will sing and give praise,
even with my glory.
PSALM 108:1

Focus your heart on the heart of God and He will work miracles in your love life. Seek to follow God's example as you relate to your loved ones. He will bless you as your mind and heart are stayed on Him.

Forgiveness

For You, Lord, are good,
and ready to forgive,
And abundant in mercy to all
those who call upon You.

PSALM 86:5

orgiveness can make the sun shine on a
marriage in trouble. It will make love sprout
and grow in ground that once seemed barren.
Don't bear grudges against your beloved.
Freely forgive.

Forgiving

Bearing with one another, and forgiving
one another, if anyone has a complaint against
another; even as Christ forgave you,
so you also must do.
COLOSSIANS 3:13

A mother's love has weak eyesight.
Faults are not readily seen, and
imperfections noticed are handled with
grace. So open your eyes wide to the
forgiving eyes of your family. Only in
openness is knowing one another possible.

Foundation

Therefore whoever hears these sayings of Mine,
and does them, I will liken him to
a wise man who built his house on the rock.
MATTHEW 7:24

*B*uild your family upon the sure foundation of a shared faith and hope in the Lord Jesus Christ. If you and your family are aiming at the same targets and moving toward the same goals, your opportunity for growth and fulfillment will be magnified many times over.

Gladness

Serve the LORD with gladness;
Come before His presence with singing.
Know that the LORD, He is God;
It is He who has made us, and not we ourselves;
We are His people and the sheep of His pasture.
<small>PSALM 100:2–3</small>

*L*et gladness surround your love and lighten the hearts of all who see the devotion you share with your family. Treat each person in your family like the priceless treasure that God has shaped and designed for you.

Grace

May the L<small>ORD</small> give you increase more and more,
You and your children.
May you be blessed by the L<small>ORD</small>,
Who made heaven and earth.
P<small>SALM</small> 115:14–15

*G*od has spread His mantle of protection over your family. He loves the ones you love even more than you do. Come to Him as a family and ask for the grace you each need to live out your days.

Gratitude

I will praise You, O LORD, with my whole heart;
I will tell of all Your marvelous works.

PSALM 9:1

$\mathcal{G}$ive praise to God and stand before the Almighty in gratitude for who He is and what He has done in your own private world. Keep your eyes focused on Him and He will give you a peace beyond understanding.

Grief

Those who sow in tears
Shall reap in joy.
He who continually goes forth weeping,
Bearing seed for sowing,
Shall doubtless come again with rejoicing,
Bringing his sheaves with him.
PSALM 126:5–6

In the life of a mother, there will be times of grief. It's okay to weep. But don't weep as those families who have no hope. The God of all creation listens to you when you mourn, and He has promised to comfort you and bless you with good things.

Heart

And we have known and believed the love
that God has for us. God is love,
and he who abides in love abides in God,
and God in him.

1 JOHN 4:16

*G*od has a cozy place for you and your
family in His fatherly heart. When you are
sad, He invites you to come to Him and
share your every burden. He will share His
heart with you and give you peace. Come
into His presence today and feel His love.

Heritage

Behold, children are a heritage from the LORD,
The fruit of the womb is a reward.
PSALM 127:3

*Y*our children are a heritage from the Lord. He has
placed your children in your care to delight you and
challenge you to grow into the person He wants you to be.

Honesty

Oh, that men would give
thanks to the LORD for His goodness,
And for His wonderful works to the children of men!
For He satisfies the longing soul,
And fills the hungry soul with goodness.
PSALM 107:8–9

When you come before God, don't pretend you are satisfied when you are not. Talk over any misunderstanding you may have about what He's doing in your life. God longs for honesty from His people who want to get to know Him more completely.

Honor

But above all, my brethren, do not swear,
either by heaven or by earth or with any other oath.
But let your "Yes" be "Yes," and
your "No," "No," lest you fall into judgment.
JAMES 5:12

Crown your life with honor. Be careful that scandal doesn't rightfully attach itself to your name. Live your life honestly and you and your family will enjoy peace in all your dealings.

Hope

For You are my hope, O Lord GOD;
You are my trust from my youth.
By You I have been upheld from birth;
You are He who took me out of my mother's womb.
My praise shall be continually of You.

<small>PSALM 71:5–6</small>

Hope is a mother's defense against many troubles in life. Exercise hope daily as you talk with your family. Pray in faith, believing God will answer your prayers. Ground your hope in His love.

Intimacy

Like an apple tree among the trees of the woods,
So is my beloved among the sons.
I sat down in his shade with great delight,
And his fruit was sweet to my taste.
Song of Solomon 2:3

*W*hen you share from the center of your heart, you give a gift beyond value to your beloved. Take time to give this greatest of all treasures to your husband. Share your heart with your lover alone. True intimacy will be your reward.

Joyful

And my soul shall be joyful in the LORD;
It shall rejoice in His salvation.

*E*mbrace your family with a joyful heart.
Be happy and delight in the smile, the kisses,
and the love of those who rule your heart.
Let the joy shine in your eyes and be evident
in the words of your mouth.

Kindness

And be kind to one another, tenderhearted,
forgiving one another,
even as God in Christ forgave you.
EPHESIANS 4:32

*K*indness must be woven through the fabric of the love you hold for your family. This thread must be strong enough to hold the more fragile emotions together. Seek to be kind to your family. Look for special ways to be gentle and sensitive. Together you can weather any storm.

Laughter

Light is sown for the righteous,
And gladness for the upright in heart.
PSALM 97:11

*L*augh joyously with your family. Lift your eyes to the sky and praise God for the light He has given to you together. He will direct you in plentiful paths. Walk them with joy and gladness.

Learning

Come to Me, all you who labor and are heavy laden,
and I will give you rest. Take My yoke upon you
and learn from Me, for I am gentle and lowly in heart,
and you will find rest for your souls.
MATTHEW 11:28–29

*B*eing a mother is a great teacher. You see your own faults more clearly when placed up against another's need. Thank God for His help as you grow into the person He wants you to be. Life is your school, and your family is one of your best teachers. Learn well today and every day.

Light

You are the light of the world.
A city that is set on a hill cannot be hidden.
Nor do they light a lamp and put it under a basket,
but on a lampstand, and it gives light
to all who are in the house.
MATTHEW 5:14-15

$\mathcal{A}$sk God to spread the light of love around the hearts of you and your family. His light will be the laser beam of truth to help you know each other in your innermost being. Delve deeply into the core of your togetherness as a family.

Like-Minded

Fulfill my joy by being like-minded,
having the same love,
being of one accord, of one mind.
PHILIPPIANS 2:2

 *L*ove brings an attitude of unity to your
family and helps you grow in a positive
direction. Decide together what is important
in the lives you share. You and your husband
are two, but your hearts must beat as one.

Listen

The hearing ear and the seeing eye,
The LORD has made them both.

PROVERBS 20:12

A mother's listening heart is a balm to a damaged relationship. Be willing to see your relationship through the eyes of those you love. God has given you ears to hear. Ask Him to help you listen wisely.

Little Things

A word fitly spoken is like apples of gold
In settings of silver.
PROVERBS 25:11

*L*ittle words spoken by a mother, like "Please forgive" or "I care," will make a big difference to your family. Don't neglect the seemingly little words; they speak richly of your special love and attention.

Losses

Be anxious for nothing, but in everything by prayer
and supplication, with thanksgiving,
let your requests be made known to God; and the
peace of God, which surpasses all understanding, will guard
your hearts and minds through Christ Jesus.
PHILIPPIANS 4:6–7

*G*od replaces your losses with good things. If you follow
Him and lose someone close to you, always remember how
much He cares, and that He has promised to fill your
aching void with a special kind of love.

Love

A new commandment I give to you,
that you love one another; as I have loved you,
that you also love one another.
John 13:34

Poets have tried for centuries to capture the essence of love. The Bible tells us quite simply that real love is caring more about others than we care about ourselves and our own needs. Be a model of selfless love in your relationships. It will be contagious.

Married

So husbands ought to love
their own wives as their own bodies;
he who loves his wife loves himself.
EPHESIANS 5:28

You married because you "fell in love." Now as your love matures, you find yourself "standing in love"—a far stronger form of affection. When you truly love, you ask, "What can I do for you?" rather than, "What are you doing for me?" Love is an "inside job"—it begins within your heart—but once it emerges, the outward expression of your affection makes a world of difference to your beloved.

Maturity

Now no chastening seems to be joyful for the present, but painful; nevertheless, afterward it yields the peaceable fruit of righteousness to those who have been trained by it.

Hebrews 12:11

As you and your family grow to maturity, you will see that it is during the really tough times that you developed your stability, resolve, and inner strength. Be comforted in your troubles, because difficulties are tools with which an all-knowing God shapes and perfects you.

Mercy

But I am like a green olive tree
in the house of God;
I trust in the mercy of God
forever and ever.
PSALM 52:8

*A*s a mother, don't try to hold your marriage together by yourself. Ask God for His grace and mercy in your union. God specializes in healing broken hearts. He brings His oil of love and kindness to thresholds where peace is in short supply.

Miracle

*Most assuredly, I say to you, he who believes in Me,
the works that I do he will do also, and greater works than
these he will do, because I go to My Father.
And whatever you ask in My name, that I will do,
that the Father may be glorified in the Son.*

JOHN 14:12–13

As a mother, reflect on the miracle of God's saving
grace through Jesus Christ. Ask Him to continue the
miracle of love He has begun inside of you. Let this day be
one of joy, fulfillment, and hope.

One Flesh

One of the joys and mysteries of life is the way in which a man and woman can become one. The two come together physically, emotionally, and spiritually. They no longer are two; they are one.

One Mind

Be of good comfort, be of one mind,
live in peace; and the God of love
and peace will be with you.
2 CORINTHIANS 13:11

*A*s a mother, seek harmony in your relationship with your loved ones. Don't take detours to total agreement. Talk about your differences until there is full understanding. Do not be afraid of a healthy compromise. Live with your family in peace.

Openness

Hear my voice according to your lovingkindness;
O LORD, revive me according to Your justice.
PSALM 119:149

Speak your emotions freely. Your love will flourish as a result of the outpouring of your heart. The same is true in your relationship with God. He wants you to tell Him how you feel. Speak your mind. Share your heart. God will listen and comfort you in all your ways.

Parenting

Two are better than one,
Because they have a good reward for their labor.
For if they fall, one will lift up his companion.
But woe to him who is alone when he falls,
For he has no one to help him up.
ECCLESIASTES 4:9–10

Some of the most challenging labor in life takes place in the home. It's difficult to be a parent without having someone else to help you in the hard times. Lean on your spouse for support in raising your children.

Partners

And if a house is divided against itself,
that house cannot stand.
MARK 3:25

A mother's responsibility is to develop a
sense of oneness with your partner in life.
Use disagreements to build your relationship
by talking about problems when they occur.
Don't let resentment build a wall between
you. If you do, it will become a wedge that
can split you apart.

Patience

But let patience have its perfect work,
that you may be perfect and complete,
lacking nothing.
JAMES 1:4

A mother's loving heart binds up hurts with a patient and forgiving spirit. When someone in your family stumbles, don't give up on that person. Everyone makes mistakes. Remember everyone in your family needs your unconditional love. Have patience and the bond you share will strengthen daily.

Peace

Depart from evil and do good;
Seek peace and pursue it.
PSALM 34:14

*R*esentment and unspoken anger slice through love.
They inflict wounds that may take a lifetime to recover.
Give up those grudges that may one day turn into cold
anger. Tell your family how you feel and seek to live
together in peace.

Pleasantness

Her ways are ways of pleasantness,
And all her paths are peace.
PROVERBS 3:17

As a mother, let God lead you into pleasant pastures. Ask Him to bring you to a quiet oasis where He may give you a time of rest in your life. Focus and reflect on the blessings God has given you.

Power

But I want you to know that the
head of every man is Christ,
the head of woman is man,
and the head of Christ is God.
1 CORINTHIANS 11:3

*P*ower and love—how do they mix? Each family needs to pray and consider how they are to relate to one another. Without love, power is harsh. When there is love there is no need for power.

Precious

How precious also are your
thoughts to me, O God!
How great is the sum of them!
<small>PSALM 139:17</small>

*G*ive the precious gift of your heart to God
first and then to your beloved. Do not hold
back. Give of yourself freely without
counting the price. You'll be rewarded over
and over for your efforts.

Pretense

The law of the LORD is perfect, converting the soul; the testimony of the LORD is sure, making wise the simple; the statutes of the LORD are right, rejoicing the heart; the commandment of the LORD is pure, enlightening the eyes.
PSALM 19:7–8

*L*ove makes mistakes. But a willingness to set things right is more important to your family than feigned perfection. When you make a mistake, be honest. Talk with your loved ones. Two-way communication unearths hidden treasure.

Prosper

Beloved, I pray that you may
prosper in all things
and be in health,
just as your soul prospers.
3 JOHN 2

*L*ift your arms to the sky and thank God for the sunshine He has given you. Every ounce of energy you have has been given to you by Him. Rejoice in the abundance of health and wealth He has given you and your family.

Provider

And He said to them, "Cast your net on the right side
of the boat, and you will find some."
So they cast, and now they were not able to draw it in
because of the multitude of fish.

JOHN 21:6

The Lord gives and the Lord takes away. God is the one who controls your destiny and your days. If you or your husband lacks anything, go to your heavenly Father and ask Him. He is pleased to provide for His children.

Pure

The words of the LORD are pure words,
Like silver tried in a furnace of earth,
Purified seven times.
You shall keep them O LORD,
You shall preserve them from this generation forever.
PSALM 12:6–7

*S*tudy the Scriptures. Meditate on God's Word. Read His promises together with your family and talk about what His divine counsel means in your everyday life. The Bible is as fresh today as when it was first given to humankind. Let it be your guide in your loving relationship with your family.

Refresh

The LORD is your keeper;
The Lord is your shade at your right hand.
The sun shall not strike you by day,
Nor the moon by night.
PSALM 121:5–6

*R*efresh yourself with the love you share with your family. Shape your love into the same kind of love God gives to you. May your affection be a shade tree during life's dry, scorching seasons.

Response

I, therefore, the prisoner of the Lord,
beseech you to walk worthy of the calling with
which you were called, with all lowliness
and gentleness, with longsuffering,
bearing with one another in love.
EPHESIANS 4:1–2

How do you handle criticism? How do you respond to inadequacies in yourself and others? Are you sensitive to the needs and ambitions of others? Let God teach you to reflect His love and understanding at home and in the workplace.

95

Safety

But whoever listens to me will dwell safely,
And will be secure, without fear of evil.
PROVERBS 1:33

*G*od promises you and your family a safe
dwelling place in Him. Bring your hurts and
disappointments to your loving Father who
wants only His best for you. Don't try to
handle life all on your own. Live your life by
living and loving together with the Lord.

Sanctuary

I will remember the works of the LORD;
Surely I will remember Your wonders of old.
I will also meditate on all Your work,
And talk of Your deeds.
Your way, O God, is in the sanctuary;
Who is so great a God as our God?
PSALM 77:11–13

*M*ake your life a sanctuary for you and your family.
Keep your relationship with your family healthy and
strong so it may be a place of comfort and retreat from
the troubles of life.

Satisfied

As for me, I will see your face in righteousness;
I shall be satisfied
when I awake in Your likeness.
PSALM 17:15

As you grow to know your husband, grow also to know the Lord who watches over both of you. Spend time meditating on God's Word. Do not be content with only surface knowledge of the Savior. Dig deeply into the riches of His presence.

Seek

Seek the LORD and His strength;
Seek His face evermore.
PSALM 105:4

As a mother, you and your family grow as you seek to know God better. Don't be content with a glimpse of Him. Search the Scriptures and yearn to see His face clearly. He'll show Himself to those who seek Him.

Seeking

The heart of the prudent acquires knowledge,
And the ear of the wise seeks knowledge.
PROVERBS 18:15

*L*ife for a mother can seem like a series of closed doors. Don't be afraid to ask to have the door opened. God wants you and your family to seek what you want and assures you that you will find it. That is His generous promise to you.

Success

Whatever your hand finds to do,
do it with your might; for there is no work
or device or knowledge or wisdom
in the grave where you are going.
ECCLESIASTES 9:10

*C*elebrate every season with those in your family. Lift your arms and give thanks. Embrace joy and happiness. God is in all good things. Applaud your family's achievements with enthusiasm and join together with them in thanksgiving.

Talent

And to one he gave five talents,
to another two, and to another one,
to each according to his own ability;
and immediately he went on a journey.
MATTHEW 25:15

Strive to look at yourself clearly. God has given you a multitude of gifts and talents. He has given similar and perhaps much different talents to your children. Encourage yourself and all your family members to develop all the talents God has given you. Do the very best with the gifts you have. They are all you'll ever need.

Tenderness

Let, I pray, Your merciful kindness be for my comfort,
According to Your word to Your servant.
Let Your tender mercies come to me, that I may live;
For Your law is my delight.
<small>PSALM 119:76–77</small>

A mother who is tender with those she loves the most will outlast difficult times. Nourish your love in the hard times. It will make your troubles more bearable. Learn to stand close to your loved ones when storms shake your household.

Thankful

Know that the LORD, He is God;
It is He who has made us, and not we ourselves;
We are His people and the sheep of His pasture.
Enter into His gates with thanksgiving,
And into His courts with praise.
Be thankful to Him, and bless His name.

Psalm 100:3–4

*A*s a mother, develop a thankful heart. Look for reasons to be thankful to God and to your mate. A thankful tongue will water your relationships until love blossoms beyond your greatest expectations.

Transgressions

For as the heavens are high above the earth,
So great is His mercy toward those who fear Him.
As far as the east is from the west,
So far has He removed our transgressions from us.
PSALM 103:11–12

Mother, if inner troubles plague your marriage, don't give up. The One who has borne all your transgressions is also the One who gives you hope for a new tomorrow.

Trust

Trust in the LORD forever,
For in YAH, the LORD, is everlasting strength.
ISAIAH 26:4

*L*et your family know they can trust in your loyalty and
fidelity. Trust is one key that begins with your relationship
with the Lord and ends with your family. Cultivate trust
and you cultivate a fulfilling and refreshing life.

Unity

Behold, how good and how pleasant it is
For brethren to dwell together in unity!
PSALM 133:1

True love knits a family together until the threads of each life are intertwined with the threads of the others. Celebrate the unity you share with each person in the family God has given you. Give thanks today—right now—by praising God for what you are sharing together.

Virtue

Who can find a virtuous wife?
For her worth is far above rubies.
PROVERBS 31:10

*V*irtue is the foundation of a solid marriage. Let your family know they can safely trust in your affection and love for them. Don't give in to the temptation to squander your love in any way.

Waiting

For the eyes of the LORD are on the righteous,
And His ears are open to their prayers.
1 PETER 3:12

*P*ray for your family with confidence that
God will give you the desires of your heart.
God listens to your pleas and your deepest
concerns. His ears are waiting to hear your
inner desires. He cares about you with an
everlasting love.

Wisdom

The father of the righteous will greatly rejoice,
And he who begets a wise child will delight in him.
Let your father and your mother be glad,
And let her who bore you rejoice.

PROVERBS 23:24–25

When you train your child well, you will bear pleasant fruit in later years. A wise and righteous child will bring joy to the hearts of you and your spouse. Encourage your child in the ways of wisdom.